GO OUTSIDE

13 Lessons Learned as a Church Planter and Re-planter

Sterling Edwards

Copyright © 2019, Sterling Edwards
Go Outside: 13 Lessons Learned as a Church Planter and Re-planter

ISBN: 978-1-945774-38-6

Trust House Publishers
P.O. Box 3181
Taos, NM 87571

www.trusthousepublishers.com

Ordering Information: Special discounts are available on quantity purchases by churches, associations, and retailers. For details, contact the publisher at the address above or call toll-free 1-844-321-4202.

1 2 3 4 5 6 7 8 9 10

Table of Contents

Introduction 1

Chapter One: God Loves People More Than I Do 3

Chapter Two: God is Faithful, Even When I Am Not 7

Chapter Three: It is His Church and Not Mine 11

Chapter Four: The Vision of the Church Was Not Mine Alone 15

Chapter Five: The Importance of a Team 19

Chapter Six: What I Said or Did as The Pastor of The Church
Did Not Matter Much to My Family 23

Chapter Seven: I Had to Learn to Evaluate My Sermon Without
Asking My Wife 29

Chapter Eight: God Does Not Love Me More or Less Based upon
The Worship Attendance on Any Given Sunday 35

Chapter Nine: 1 Comes Before 100 39

Chapter Ten: Leading with Authenticity Is Better Than Leading
with Authority 43

Chapter Eleven: "His Grace Is Enough" 45

Chapter Twelve: God Works in Me Before He Works Through Me 49

Chapter Thirteen: Life Is an Adventure and I Would not Change a Thing 55

About the Author 59

Introduction

Our family moved to New York exactly thirteen years ago today – July 5, 2006. At the time, Madison was 8 years old, Emma was 3 years old, and there was not yet an Avery or a Charlotte.

Our journey began when First Baptist Church in Katy, Texas, had a vision and plan to help establish a new church on Long Island. The church, in partnership with the North American Mission Board, made a commitment to support our family as we made the move from Houston, Texas, to Long Island, New York.

We arrived in Levittown, New York, not knowing anyone and honestly not knowing that much about how to get started.

Because of my upbringing, I at least thought that I had an idea of what church was supposed to look like. I grew up attending church. My Dad was a pastor, and my Mom played the piano and lead the children's choir. However, I soon realized that my previous experiences in church were very different from the present reality of moving to a place where there were not as many churches.

We knew that the move from Houston was a big deal. It felt monumental and significant. But we could have never known, then, how our lives would be changed forever.

It is humbling to look back and realize what we did not know and to see all the ways that God was faithful in spite of us. It is also very surreal to think of how quickly the time has gone and all that has transpired over these 13 years.

I still do not have all the answers. Truthfully, I know more about what not to do. Yet, we have seen the power of God on display in numerous ways during our time here. We have seen people changed and transformed. We have seen marriages resurrected. We have seen addicts recover. We have seen people trust Jesus and surrender their lives to Him.

As I look back on this journey, I realize that I had a front row seat to seeing the hand of God work in ways that were beyond my imagination. But I also very much recognize that I can take zero credit for all that has taken place. As much as it can seem like we were doing the work, making the connections, and investing our time, the reality is that we were still a part of the audience watching God demonstrate His power and His strength.

I have compiled a list of 13 things that I have learned over these last 13 years in planting and replanting churches in New York. This list is not comprehensive, and I may add to this list in the future. Just as easily, I could write an entire other list of the top 13 mistakes that were made. I may get to that one eventually. But, for now, this book consists of 13 lessons that I have learned over these last 13 years in New York.

I pray that this will be a blessing and encouragement. More than anything, I pray that this book would be a testimony to God's grace, God's love, and God's power.

Thank you.

-Sterling

CHAPTER ONE

God Loves People More Than I Do

Within the first month of moving to Levittown, New York, I began having serious doubts about how we were supposed to go about planting a new church. I knew that it involved starting a church. I knew that the church that we planted was supposed to be established and healthy. But I did not know where or how to actually begin starting a new church.

At the beginning, we were told to get our family settled and get to know our community which seemed simple enough. We unpacked and unboxed all our belongings and arranged the furniture and all the rooms a few times. Eventually, we were settled. Yet, we were still left with trying to figure out where to begin as it pertained to starting the church.

After living in New York for a couple of weeks, we ventured to our local Home Depot in East Meadow to look for a stove for our kitchen. It was here that we were introduced to Carol, and it was here that we first caught a glimpse of how God was already at work.

Carol worked in the appliance section of Home Depot. She politely asked us if she could help us. We responded that we were just looking, but our very brief statement was more than enough for her detect that we were not from New York.

Maybe it was our vocabulary. Maybe it was our accents. In any case, Carol asked us where we were from. We told Carol that we had just moved from Texas. Inevitably, she wanted to know why. Almost sheepishly, I told her that we had moved to New York in order to start a new church. I was hoping that she would not press me about any details because I had no idea what any of those details were. At the moment, it was difficult to envision even having something that I could invite Carol to attend.

My church experience up to this point had involved making a connection and inviting someone to a Bible study, small group, worship service, fellowship, or some type of event taking place at the church building or somewhere related to the church. Nonetheless, I let Carol know that we had moved to Long Island to start a church. Other than that one truthful fact, I did not even know what I could tell her or anything at all that we had to offer her.

Jenna and I quietly stood there waiting, bracing ourselves for Carol's response. We could not help but wonder if she was going to think we were crazy.

It was an unusually long pause, but eventually, Carol did respond. However, Carol did not respond with the questions or the cynicism that we were anticipating. In a very calm and relaxed manner, she closed her eyes and said, "I have been praying that God would give me a pastor."

This was not at all the response we were expecting. I would have been amazed if Carol had said that she was praying that God would show her a church. That would have made sense to me; I could have imagined that.

But that is not what she said. In a moment, God was changing my understanding about what we were doing in New York. He was blowing up the paradigm of church that I had held onto for so long while simultaneously opening my eyes to a greater understanding of Who He was and what He wanted to do with me.

I walked out of the Home Depot with a sense of conviction, but also excitement. Up to that point, I had been looking to establish a church the way I thought it was supposed to look. But instead, God was showing me that He loves all people – every single person.

Over the next couple of days, God would use the quick and simple conversation with Carol to change my heart and my mind. It was then that I began to understand the truth that God loves people more than I do and that His desire for people to know Him is even greater than my own.

It is easy to think that telling someone about the love of God rests on our shoulders. This makes it easy to feel overwhelmed and burdened to carry the weight of communicating God's love. We can worry about their response. We can worry they will misunderstand us. We can worry that we will come across as judgmental, legalistic, and self-righteous. But God showed me something incredibly important during those first few months living in Levittown that lightened the heavy burden I was carrying.

God loves people more than me, and He wants people to know His love more than I do. I had nothing to invite Carol to attend from our non-existent church. Yet, the Lord quickly revealed to me that I was now Carol's pastor. Over the next year, I went to the Home Depot thirty-five times. If Carol was there, I would pray with her. If Carol was not there, I would stand in the middle of some refrigerators and pray for her. In later years, Carol would attend our worship services, and I would drink coffee in Carol's home. But, an incredible part of my journey in New York began at that Home Depot in East Meadow.

Within the first month of living in New York, I learned that it never was about trying to get people to come "my" thing. I was not going to be the Savior; I was not the answer. Ultimately, that first month of living in New York allowed for me to learn that sharing the message of God's Love was way more about me going than people coming.

God has already demonstrated the full extent of His love for people by sending Jesus to die for every single one of us. Further, He has demonstrated His love by sending us, as followers of Jesus, to share the truth of His love. God wants people to know about His love even more than we do, but we get to be the ones that go and share His love with others.

But God proves his own love for us in that while
we were still sinners, Christ died for us.
Romans 5:8

CHAPTER TWO

God is Faithful, Even When I Am Not

When it comes to beginning a new church in a new place, it is easier to become aware of just how much God's power and intervention is needed. It is not that His power and intervention are not needed in every church, but there is a very real desperation at the outset of starting a church.

When we first started a new church in East Islip, I would pace outside of the theater that we were renting on Sunday evenings, hoping and praying that someone would come to a worship gathering. It was in some of these moments that I began to have two types of conversations with God. More accurately stated, these were probably conversations I was having with myself.

In my longing to see people attend our new church plant, I would lay out my list of the things that I had done to try and get this church started. I would recount the efforts. I would recount the time. I would recount the investment. I would desperately try to convince God of the reasons why there should have been people showing up to our new church.

This type of conversation took place on the good days. On the not so good days, I would pace outside of the theater plagued by my guilt and recount my other list. I would recall what I had not done. I would recount my lack of effort, my lack of engagement, and my lack of prayer. I would desperately try to negotiate promises to God on what I would do in the future, if He could just send some people to show up to our new church.

Let me stop right here and state that is impossible for me to adequately emphasize just how dangerous and sinful this way of thinking is. This mindset is in no way rooted in an accurate understanding of who God is and how God works. Even further, it is not rooted in an accurate understanding of who we are.

The success, or lack thereof, concerning the new church we were planting was not an indicator of God's love for me or the people in our community. However, it becomes very easy to personalize these things and base our own self-worth on the current condition of our church.

Again, I cannot overstate how dangerous and deceitful it is to think this way. It is not true nor is it accurate on any level. It took me a while to grasp hold of the amazing truth that God is faithful, even when I am not faithful. I had to remember that His unchanging love never fails and His all-sufficient grace is always enough.

The truth about the extent of God's love in no way discounts the effort, work, and investment that is needed from us. Planting, re-planting, and pastoring a church requires us to give our all. However, there is absolute freedom in knowing that God is faithful, even when we do not do it all perfectly. God demonstrates His power beyond our own efforts and is sovereign over our insufficiencies. He knows more than we do and he knows what we do not know. Additionally, God provides what we do not have and leads when we do not know where to go.

Personally, I have seen God's faithfulness despite my insufficiencies. This is not me offering some type of false humility nor a situation in which I am beating myself up needlessly - not at all. My friend Steve Canter always says that "church planting will expose your greatest weakness." And I know this to be true. There are things that I have I done and decisions that I have made that I would love to have the chance to do over again.

Over the years, I have made decisions that hurt people, injured friendships, and caused pain in ways that I never intended. There have been numerous times when I have made the wrong call or the wrong decision. While I do have regret and remorse about these things, I can also share that I have seen God's grace toward me all along the way.

There have been enough of those decisions where I can now look back and see how God, in spite of me, demonstrated His power and authority. I can now see how God has remained faithful every step of the way, even when I made the wrong call. And I can now see a very real truth that every church planter and pastor must embrace: We are all inadequate to build God's church. As long as this is up for debate, the struggle will wear us down and the Enemy will take us out. We should not try to plant a healthy church in our own power and strength because we cannot plant a healthy church in our own power and strength.

Above all, we must remember that God is faithful even when we are not.

if we are faithless, he remains faithful, for he cannot deny himself.

2 Timothy 2:13

CHAPTER THREE

It is His Church and Not Mine

Within a couple of weeks of moving to Long Island, we opened up a post office box for the mail that we anticipated we would receive, for the church we anticipated we would start. It did not take many visits to the post office for me to become acquainted with some of clerks who were working at this particular branch.

Christina was one of the clerks. She was genuinely interested in the fact that we were beginning a new church. She was a follower of Jesus and regularly wanted to know the progress about the church we were beginning. This is one of my earliest memories of hearing someone refer to the church we were starting as "your church." Christina would ask, "How is your church coming along?" "When is your church going to meet?" "What kind of music does your church have?"

It really is not that uncommon to have someone ask anyone else about his or her church and refer to it as "your church." What is your church like? Does your church do this or have that? Yet, subtly, there can be a shift in the level of ownership assumed in the church by the pastor or church planter. We can begin to take on any and all responsibilities. We can begin to assume the identity as someone who is in charge and calling the shots. It is not as if a pastor or church planter wakes up one morning and declares himself to be the CEO of his church. Nor do we necessarily take on the titles of president and owner of our churches. But, I have seen it come pretty close to this.

Depending upon the status of a church or a church plant, the pastor or church planter takes on tremendous responsibilities and often carries a disproportionate amount of these responsibilities, especially in the early stages of a church plant. Leadership, vision, preaching, finances, outreach, partnerships, and pastoral care are some of the tasks that the pastor or church planter is responsible for carrying out. With all of these responsibilities, it becomes second nature to bring any and all questions revolving around any aspect of the church to the pastor.

While establishing leadership and distributing some of the responsibilities to others is essential, there is still a tendency for some of us who are pastors to "own" everything. There is often a mindset in us that says that if I do not do it, it will not get done. There are times when we think that we cannot ask someone else to take something on. We may think that we can do it faster; maybe we even think we can do it better. Either way, we do it ourselves rather than seeking out the help of someone else.

Please do not misunderstand this way of thinking. It does not necessarily come out of a heart of selfishness or from being extremely territorial. There is a part of this that comes from a sincere desire to serve and also from the belief that, as pastors, we are not above serving in any way that is needed. We want to think that we are willing to do whatever we ask someone else to do. Yet, this can be a slippery slope. The truth is, we cannot do everything, nor are we supposed to do everything.

I remember one night in Farmingdale, when we were preparing to host a mission team. I was tired and weary. I should also add that my heart and attitude were probably not operating at full capacity. On this particular night, I remember being frustrated at things that were going on at home. I was rushing to fulfill my responsibilities as a husband and father, but my head was focused on the mission team that would be coming into LaGuardia Airport late that night.

I was highly anticipating the arrival of this mission team in particular because I desperately wanted to form a partnership with the church from which this team was coming. I knew that our church needed some help financially, and I had put my hope in the fact that a partnership with this church would fix and eliminate all of my concerns and worries. In an effort to make a good impression on this mission team, I went over to the church building where this group would be staying and made preparations for the team to have a welcoming and comfortable place to stay. I blew up and put sheets on all of their air mattresses, put the pillow cases on all of their pillows, folded all of their blankets, and placed the blankets at the foot of each air mattress. I even put a piece of chocolate on every pillow.

Now, please understand, there was a very significant part of me that was sincerely trying to serve this mission team. I did care about the people that were coming to help serve with us for the upcoming week. But there was also an underlying motive that was not good and was not healthy.

I had taken on the responsibility of spending hours on something that these individuals could have accomplished in ten minutes. This is one example of dozens and dozens of times when I have not properly shared the responsibility.

It is very easy to get wrapped up in thinking that everything at the church hinges on you. Usually, this mindset is something that starts out innocently enough. It often begins in the form of service and an attitude that reflects a willingness to do whatever it takes. Yet, for many of us, it can easily turn into a belief that we are personally responsible for everything and everybody. This can quickly result in an environment where we end up taking the credit for everything that goes right. On the flip side, we can just as easily begin carrying the blame for everything that goes wrong.

The point is, the church does not actually belong the pastor. The church belongs to the Lord.

This one issue of the ownership of the church has taken out many well-intentioned pastors and church planters. It is essential for each pastor to know that our identity is not found in the things that go right or the things that go wrong in a church.

As much as I loved the church, cared about the church, and was invested in the church, it was crucial for me to learn that it was absolutely His church and not mine. God cares about people more than we care about people. God loves His church more than we love His church. We cannot elevate ourselves above Him. Nor we can elevate ourselves over anyone else. Therefore, we must be willing to share our responsibilities with others when we can, and ultimately, we must be willing to trust God in the building of His church.

Unless the Lord builds the house, those who build it labor in vain.

Psalm 127:1

CHAPTER FOUR

The Vision of the Church Was Not Mine Alone

Within the first couple of months of moving to Long Island, I found a Qdoba Burrito Restaurant. Growing up in Texas, I was practically raised on burritos, so this was a big deal to me.

My first visit to the Qdoba in Hicksville, New York was one I will never forget. I was finishing my lunch and reading my Bible, when a man came up to my table and introduced himself as Art. I introduced myself as well, and after a couple of moments of small pleasantries, Art saw my Bible opened. He asked me if I was a Christian. When I told him that I was, he enthusiastically said that he was as well. Art then asked me if I was pastor. I told him that I was and that we had just recently moved from Texas to start a church. Art smiled and said, "That's great! I just moved from Dallas to open a burrito restaurant!"

I was extremely glad that he thought we had something in common and that I was able to make a connection with someone in the burrito business. I told Art a little more about our plans to start a church and Art was genuinely interested. After I gave him the five-minute version of our story, he nodded his head approvingly. Then Art said, "Anytime you have someone that you want to take to lunch or dinner from your church, you can always bring them here, and it will always be on me."

Art was a great encouragement to me the first couple of years that we were in New York. And during that time, I brought dozens of people to lunch at his restaurant. Art gave me a lot of credibility with the people that I was meeting with thanks to his "if you are a friend of Sterling, you are a friend of mine, it's on the house" dialogue. Art also contributed financially to the church, and one weekend he even lent me his Porsche convertible to take Jenna out to dinner.

Art, as well as many other people along the way, appreciated the vision that we had to start a new church. We have met people in New York and outside of New York who believed in the vision of starting a new church to share the message of Jesus to people in our community.

During my thirteen years here in New York, we have been extraordinarily blessed by people who have invested time, energy, and finances into Crossroads Church of Long Island and Park Slope Community Church in Brooklyn. We have seen hundreds of thousands of dollars given by churches and individuals to help these churches stabilize and grow. We have also seen thousands of people who have come to New York to serve to serve on short-term mission trips and dozens of people who have moved to New York for different periods of time to serve with our church.

It is incredibly humbling to think of the churches and supporters who have given sacrificially to help these churches and to demonstrate love toward the people of Long Island and Brooklyn over these years. Yet, all of this is because they shared the vision of seeing people changed and transformed by Jesus.

Ultimately, I came to realize and recognize the real vision was not just mine. It was not just the vision of First Baptist Church of Katy, Texas, nor of the North American Mission Board. I humbly came to see that God had a vision and plan for people coming to know Him. God had a desire to see people changed and transformed. And when it is a God-sized vision, with His fingerprints all over it, it is not that hard for people to share a vision. So, no, the vision for our church was not mine to own, but it was definitely mine to share.

> *The Lord does not delay his promise, as some understand delay, but is patient with you, not wanting any to perish but all to come to repentance.*
>
> 2 Peter 3:9

CHAPTER FIVE

The Importance of a Team

I have always appreciated the game of baseball. Growing up, I was a Houston Astros fan, and I have rooted for the Mets for the last thirteen years in New York. I like that baseball has nine position players on defense that have a designated area to cover and that there is as much need for a second basemen as there is a right fielder. There is no position that is insignificant. Baseball has many dimensions, but the idea that it is truly a team sport resonates with me in a strong way.

From the beginning of our time in New York, we learned the importance and significance of serving as a team. One person cannot do everything. Two people cannot do everything. When we brought on our first additional staff member at our church, someone remarked, "What on earth could two grown men do to stay busy for an entire week at a church this size?"

It turns out, that was never a problem. We found a way to stay busy. In fact, we had more to do than we could handle. But it was not only about getting the job done. We saw how God brought together different people from different backgrounds. We also saw how He lead people who were gifted in different areas to join us on our team at just the right time. God orchestrated people together who were very different, yet were focused on the singular goal of seeing people come to know Jesus.

One of my favorite memories of serving at Crossroads Church of Long Island was having a weekly meeting with Luis Rivera and John Zizolfo. In the early days of Crossroads, every single Monday, John would walk into our office with Dunkin' Donuts coffee. We never ordered the coffee and he never asked.

One particular Monday, we were talking through the prospect of beginning a new church in East Islip, New York. We presented and discussed a few things. I wrote some information on the white board. The three of us then stared at one another in silence, while sipping our Dunkin' Donuts coffee.

John broke the silence, and Luis and I made eye contact. In his Long Island Italian accent, John said, "Listen. I want to tell you both something. There is a target on your backs. There is an Enemy who wants to take you out. This is serious business. We are going to pray, then we are going to pray, then we are going to pray." Luis and I nodded in agreement knowing that John's words were so true. After weeks of praying, we concluded that there was no way we were going to start a new church without some more help.

Around that time, we had been talking to a wonderful couple from Texas who was interested in serving at Crossroads and helping the church take some much needed next steps. Steve and Rosie Scott were willing to make the move to New York and serve in our church. All we needed to do was find a place for them to live.

Within a week, Jenna and I as well as our kids were having dinner with John and his wife, Sue. At dinner that night, John and Sue told us that they had talked about and decided that we could live at their house. They would move to the upstairs apartment while we would live on the main level, allowing Steve and Rosie to live at the church parsonage. This proposal set events in motion that would lead to a new church being started in East Islip, provide significant help for our team, and bring about substantial growth for our church.

This demonstration of teamwork is one example out of hundreds showing the willingness of people to come together and serve together. Over the years, we have been privileged to have numerous people who invested their lives to serve with us. Every single person and every single family who has served with us has made some significant sacrifice, all for the sake of seeing people come to know Jesus.

Honestly, it is humbling to look back and see how God has orchestrated His plan by bringing a team of people together to provide the leadership that is needed. And I am so grateful for all of the people that I have been privileged to serve alongside over these last thirteen years.

It is not always easy to lead a team, but it is crucial to surround ourselves with leaders who are willing to give, serve, commit, and grow with the church. I will confess that I did not always lead our team in the right way. There were times when I said yes when I should have said no. There were times when I said no when I should have said yes. There are times when I did not communicate, appreciate, and empower the people who were willing to serve in the right way. This would certainly be on my list of things that I would do differently. Yet, I know that the hearts of every person that I have been privileged to serve alongside were doing what they were doing unto the Lord, and I will forever be truly honored to have had the opportunity to serve alongside so many outstanding people over these last thirteen years.

> *Let us hold on to the confession of our hope without wavering, since he who promised is faithful. And let us watch out for one another to provoke love and good works, 25 not neglecting to gather together, as some are in the habit of doing, but encouraging each other, and all the more as you see the day approaching.*
>
> Hebrews 10:23-24

CHAPTER SIX

What I Said or Did as The Pastor of The Church Did Not Matter Much to My Family

At the beginning of our time in New York, there was a wise pastor from Texas named Harold Sellers who would regularly check in on me. On multiple occasions, Brother Harold would share some words and insight about church planting and the importance of connecting with people in a community. But, to be certain, Harold's emphasis was also on making certain that I prioritized my family.

Brother Harold would ask about Jenna and the kids in all of our conversations. At the time, I was probably responding more with, "Yeah, yeah, yeah. Everybody is good." I was probably more interested and excited to talk about the other components of starting a new church. Yet, Brother Harold continually let me know that my family was the first priority. It is not that I did not believe Brother Harold. It is not that I did not love and appreciate my family. But there are times when they were not the priority that they should have been despite Brother Harold's warnings and admonition.

Unfortunately, there are some areas of my life where I tend to be a slow learner. So, it took me a while to clearly see and recognize that the leadership of my family was not connected in any way to my leadership of the church and that my status as a pastor and church planter had little impact on my relationship with my wife and children.

Over the course of my life and ministry, I have been taught and I have learned the importance of prioritizing God, my family, and my life in general. Most of the time, the idea of what my priorities should look like was illustrated by having God as my first priority, followed by my family, and then followed by ministry. That looks good on paper. But over time, I became confused about how these priorities played out in my life. Or to put it more bluntly, I know what it is to have my priorities out of place.

It seemed that I was able to accomplish many tasks for God, with God, and because of God, in the name of ministry. Furthermore, it seemed that there were aspects of my decision-making as a pastor, that were direct results of my relationship with God.

Serving, discipleship, and evangelism were a part of my relationship with God, but also a part of my ministry. My ministry was not an add-on or addendum to my life. My ministry was directly linked to my calling from God. But, because ministry and my personal relationship with God are so closely intertwined, at various times, it has been easy for me to prioritize my responsibilities as a minister over my responsibilities as a husband and father.

This was almost never intentional. As a matter of fact, most of the time, I would deny any implications of the sort. The shift in my priorities was subtle at first. I would dwell on a particular criticism and try to overcome that feeling of insufficiency by attempting to make myself look better in some other way. On the other hand, I would dwell on a particular compliment, finding my worth and value in those words. Yet, while my priorities were becoming less focused, it was still possible to claim that what I was doing was in the name of God.

Slowly, my ministry took priority over my marriage. I began to value what others said and thought more than I should have, and I began to believe that people needed me specifically. So, I lived as though it were up to me to solve and fix the problems of other people.

Because of this thinking, I would carry the weight of the success or failure of the church on my shoulders. In an unhealthy way, I even began to think that God needed me. This led me to somehow think that if I did or did not do something, I would either be letting God down or making God look better. I was able to justify thinking and feeling this way, but this mentality was truly deceptive, leading to an unrealistic view of myself, of others, and of God. There is no question about it, pride had taken over as priority number one.

The thing is, at the time, I never would have admitted that this was the case. I would have stuck to my story that God was my first priority, followed by my family and, then, my ministry. The lack of proper priorities began to take a toll on our marriage. I specifically remember wanting Jenna to validate me and see me the way that I thought everyone else did. I was not even seeing myself with accuracy, but I thought Jenna should be seeing me in a different light. I even remember going so far as to try and prove my value and my worth to Jenna. There were a couple of moments that I would actually use a point from my sermon as a chance to prove something to Jenna or to illustrate my righteousness. Instead, this illustrated just how much my priorities were out of place.

After some time, some Godly intervention from a few trusted friends, and some grace from an incredibly gracious wife who would not give in to my delusions, I specifically remember the Holy Spirit convicting me. I remember the gentle, but direct way that the Holy Spirit spoke to my heart.

After this, things began coming back into focus. The priorities and lack of priorities returned to their proper places. I was learning that nothing that I ever said in a sermon was ever going to impact my wife or my daughters more than what I did during the other 167 hours of the week. Nothing that I did in my ministry could possibly substitute or excuse being less attentive, loving, and caring as a husband or father. However, God was showing me that being the husband and father that God had called me to be and intended for me to be would certainly validate and authenticate my life in ministry.

As I was learning that it was imperative to lead at home before I lead in ministry, I also recognized that it was necessary that my wife and children know that I love and value them more than anything that someone says, more than what anyone else thinks, and more than my own attempts at perceived success.

Finally, I have realized that I have nothing that God has not entrusted to me. If I cannot care for the family that He has entrusted to me, I must not think that I can somehow care more about other relationships that He has entrusted to me. In an effort to lead my family and love my family, I have to be able to keep my priorities straight. That means that I cannot become captured by the applause of others, nor is it okay for me to dwell on the criticism of others. I cannot take my calling lightly, nor can I falsely think that I am the only one that God can use.

God allowed for me to clearly see that my love for Him is demonstrated at home, every bit as much as it is anywhere else. My priorities are demonstrated in the way that I live and love more than in any sermon I preach or anything else I say. I want to live out each of these priorities. Yet, I have learned that living out these priorities is not simply done by making a list of these priorities.

Living out my priorities stems from me daily recognizing, daily admitting, and daily confessing my dependence upon God, my desperate need for His grace, and my gratitude for the extent of His love. Coming to the end of myself allows me to clearly see what my real priorities are. Otherwise, pride will always cause me to completely distort my view of God, my family, other people, and myself. Yes, I could say that my family was my top priority. But they needed more from me. My family needs me to lead them, not preach to them. My family needs me to love them, not perfect them. And my family needs me to look at them, not plan for them.

What I said or did as the pastor of the church did not matter to my family. This statement makes it sound like my family did not care about what was going on at our church. Nothing could have been further from the truth. They did. They not only cared, but they were fully invested in all facets of the church. However, I had to learn the hard way that any of my activities and responsibilities as a pastor and church planter did not substitute for being a husband and a father. I had to learn that my sermon on Sunday was not the content to lead my family. Jenna and Madison, especially, have helped me to learn that the best way for me to lead our family had nothing to do with my titles or my responsibilities from the church but had everything to do with the way I lived with and loved them in our daily lives.

One last word about family and ministry. Every pastor needs a Harold Sellers in his life. I have been blessed to have a couple of key men who have spoken into me on the right day and the right time, as well as on the wrong day and wrong time. I am old enough now to have the opportunity to be a Brother Harold to a few guys. And I never want to stop looking for the Brother Harold in my life or being a Brother Harold in someone else's life. There is no one in any ministry who does not need this. There is an ongoing battle to destroy our family. As John Zizolfo says, there is a target on our backs. The Enemy knows that if He can destroy our family, in many cases, the church will go right down with it. We have seen this happen numerous times and in numerous ways. And yet, if the family is strong, we often see the church thrive in ways beyond what we could have imagined.

> *Iron sharpens iron, and one person sharpens another.*
>
> Proverbs 27:17

CHAPTER SEVEN

I Had to Learn to Evaluate My Sermon Without Asking My Wife

In the early stages of our church plant, I would regularly ask Jenna her thoughts about my sermon. There were not always a lot of people that could provide me with feedback. Truthfully, I did not always want to hear the feedback that others may have offered. Still, it would be hard to count how many times I have said the words, "So what did you think?" to Jenna following a sermon.

Maybe we were in the car, maybe we had just sat down to lunch, or maybe we were still at the church. Regardless of where we were, there have been hundreds of times that I have asked for feedback regarding a sermon that I had just preached. There are many aspects of preaching that are so important and so vital to our ministry, so how we communicate does matter. It is of tremendous significance that what we say and how we say it is done in a manner that reflects the gospel we are trying to proclaim. Still, I had to learn that I could not constantly bombard Jenna with the task of evaluating my sermon every Sunday.

To avoid always asking Jenna the same questions, it became important for me to acknowledge a few things that were true for every Sunday, no matter the content of the sermon.

Every time that we get up to preach, we are aware of the fact that:

- There are people who hear my sermons weekly, and there are also people who are attending a worship service for the first time sitting in the same room.

- There are people who are celebrating, and there are people who are hurting that are sitting next to one another.

- There are people who have tremendous biblical knowledge, and there are people who have no biblical knowledge sitting within a few feet of one another.

- No two Sundays are exactly the same.

With those facts established, I began to prepare my sermons acknowledging these statements. Regardless of the text that we are preaching, each pastor must navigate through these factors. The complexity of these circumstances is what often has prompted me to get my wife's feedback. But, over the years, I have found that seeking my wife's feedback was not the only way or the best way for me to honestly evaluate my sermons.

Here are five questions that I have used to help me effectively evaluate a sermon.

1. Was the sermon true to the text I was preaching?

We want to proclaim what the Bible passage is communicating. Yet, there are times when we may be tempted to angle a verse to help us make a particular point that is not actually found in the Bible verse.

When we preach for our own purposes or for our own agenda, we will always feel incomplete at the conclusion of a sermon.

2. Was the sermon true in my life?

One of the surest ways to feel insecure about the sermon that we have just preached is to try and convey a truth from God's Word that does not match up with the present realities of our own lives. No one ever stands up to preach in perfection or without sin. Yet, we must also have wrestled with conviction and repentance of the truth of God's Word before we share this truth with others.

3. What was the response of the people to the sermon I was preaching?

This can be somewhat of a tricky question. Just because ten people came up to us after the sermon to tell us how good the sermon was, does not always mean that the sermon was good. Just because ten people complained about the sermon does not always mean that the sermon was bad. When it comes to verbal responses following our sermon, we must be careful not to give either applause or criticism too much weight. Yet, our sermons should lead to some level of response. They should lead people to affirm the Truth of God's Word when they hear it and move or motivate them to repent, pray, give, and go.

4. What did my wife or someone else hear?

The advantage to having my wife to evaluate my sermon is that she will give it to me straight. If I ask, I do not ever have to wonder what she is thinking. But I have learned not to ask my wife, "What did you think?" following a sermon. And I have decided that I did not want to always burden her with the role of being my personal sermon evaluator since she is always listening to my sermons. If there was something that stood to out her that needed to be addressed or if the sermon was exceptionally good, she would definitely let me know. Yet, I do believe that it is helpful for each of us to have a person or two people who listen to our sermons on a regular basis to provide us some feedback. We may want to ask the person who is helping us evaluate our sermon the following questions:

- Was there any part of the sermon that was confusing?

- Was there any part of the sermon that was contradicting?

- Was there any part of the sermon that did not point to the conclusion?

5. Was the sermon an offering of worship unto the Lord?

I love preaching. I love preparing and processing through the sermon as it unfolds in my heart. However, preaching a sermon is not always easy, and in many ways, preaching can be exhausting.

Yet, over the years, I have come to appreciate the fact that preparing a sermon and delivering a sermon is something extraordinarily precious and valuable. It is an absolute expression of my love and worship of my Savior. This question has changed the way that I think and the way that I approach the evaluation of my sermon. I want my sermon to be such an expression of my devotion and worship that I no longer judge my sermon by the number of people who were in the room. I no longer look at the sermon as wishing that so and so would have been present to hear it. It is simply presented and preached as on offering to the Lord.

Preach the word; be ready in season and out of season; rebuke, correct, and encourage with great patience and teaching.

2 Timothy 4:2

CHAPTER EIGHT

God Does Not Love Me More or Less Based upon The Worship Attendance on Any Given Sunday

In Chicago in the 1930's, the Cubs would indicate whether their baseball game had been won or lost by putting out a particular flag. If Cubs won, they would put out a white flag marked with a blue "W." If the Cubs lost, they would put out a blue flag marked with a white "L."

There have been plenty of Sundays when I went home from a worship service feeling like there was a flag flying to indicate whether the service was a "W" or an "L." And there are often small things that we point to in order to tell us whether the worship service was a "W" or an "L." These can include incorrect spelling on the screen, a hissing noise in the sound system or a late or absent children's ministry leader. In reality, it is usually not too hard to find things to criticize in a worship service.

But, for many of us, the attendance is a key indicator. If there were more people than the previous Sunday, by all means, fly the "W" flag. If there were fewer people than the previous Sunday, there are times that we are ready to fly the "L" flag.

But, for me, the attendance of a worship service would at times go beyond determining which flag to fly. There are times when I took the attendance very personal. It was as if my identity and self-worth could have been tied to how many people attended on a particular Sunday.

There is a strange irony with pastoring a church and planting a church. We truly want to do all that we can to make the church plant as successful as it can be. Yet, we readily acknowledge that we cannot take the credit. In his book, It's Personal, Brian Bloye says, "When the church plant doesn't do well, we take the blame. When it's successful, it's all glory to God." There have been countless Sundays when I walked out of the church feeling like a failure if the attendance was lower than average. But over the years, I have had to learn and remember that God's love for me and his church has nothing to do with attendance, offerings, or sermons.

On one particular Sunday in Brooklyn, I was discouraged by the lack of attendance. My discouragement was based on the fact that the previous Sunday had a larger attendance. It was one of the Sundays when I thought we could fly the "W" flag on the steeple of the church. But, on this Sunday, we were missing about half of the people that had been present the previous Sunday.

Even as I was preaching, I was going through the names in my head of the people who were missing. I know how terrible it sounds that I could be focused more who was not there than who was there.

As the worship service concluded, I was the only person left at the church. If there was an "L" flag handy, I would have hoisted it up right then and there.

After everyone had cleared the building, I stood at the top of the steps of the church looking out over 12th street. I was lamenting over something or another when I made eye contact with an elderly man walking down the sidewalk. He motioned to me and wanted to know if he could come in the church and look around the sanctuary.

In the ten minutes that he was in the church, I found out that he was a retired professor from France who had come to Brooklyn to visit his daughter and new grandson. This one encounter lead to meeting an amazing family that would end up attending our church and that we would come to know and love wholeheartedly.

I do not look back at that day and try to evaluate the sermon. I really have no idea how many people were there. But I do know that God was at work that day and God was making Himself known no matter what the attendance was.

The Chicago Cubs no longer indicate a win with the "W" and a loss with the "L." They fly the "W" flag all day, every day. The "W" has come to represent the team, not just a victory. I believe this is the attitude that we need for our worship services every Sunday. The "W" is not how many people who show up. The "W" is that the presence of the Lord is in our churches. The "W" is that God still offers His grace, that God still gives us His love, and that God still forgives, still restores, and still redeems. It is not always easy to break ourselves from finding our identity in the number of people in attendance. But it is certainly not an indicator of God's love for us as pastors nor of God's love for His people. Because of who He is and what He has done, we can rest in the truth that every day we can fly the "W" flag.

But thanks be to God, who gives us the victory through our Lord Jesus Christ!

1 Corinthians 15:57

CHAPTER NINE

1 Comes Before 100

One Sunday, I was asked to preach at a church on Long Island. The pastor's mother had become ill, and at the last minute, the pastor asked if I could fill in for him. I brought Emma along with me for support. She and I sat on the front row of the church. There was one person sitting directly behind us, and there were three other people on the back row. About halfway through the music, another couple showed up and sat somewhere in the middle.

As I stood up to preach, I resisted walking up on the stage. I figured everyone could just as easily see me and hear me while standing at the front of the room on the floor, so that is what I started to do. I was quickly informed, however, that the preacher preaches from the stage. Somewhat reluctantly, I took my place on the stage behind the podium to preach to the seven people in attendance, including Emma.

Any pastor will tell you that it is much easier to preach to one hundred people than to ten people. As church planters, we often have such a strong desire to want to see growth. We want to see success and we want to see it now. We desperately want to see all the chairs filled up with people, and we look forward to having the problems and headaches of dealing with parking and multiple services.

But, in our longing for the masses of people, it can become way too easy to lose sight of the individual person. It can be easy to lose our perspective that if God has entrusted us to preach to seven people, we are just as privileged and honored to proclaim the gospel as if were preaching to seven hundred. In our desire to see masses of people, we can easily overlook the individuals that God has placed right in front of us. We must be careful to not try to reach people with a bulk mentality. Instead, we need to remember that these are individuals with names and stories, and we must focus on being faithful with who is in front of us. We cannot discount or dismiss a smaller congregation in hopes of having a larger one.

For years, I have had a theme song playing in my head. I regularly play the song audibly. But the song stays in my head most of the time. My cousin, Robbie Seay, wrote a song with his band entitled "Go Outside." It can be found on their "Give Yourself Away" album. Every lyric to this resonates with me. But there are six words to this song that I feel like have operated as my personal soundtrack for the last dozen years. The words found in the are "No one should be left out." Do yourself a favor and listen to this song. I admit, I am partial to nearly all of Robbie's songs. Yet, I cannot think of too many songs that have impacted me like this song has.

The understanding that "no one should be left out" is the theme of the gospel. It is for every single person. It is for the person who grew up in church and for the person who did not grow up in church. It is for the person who has been faithful and for the person who has been faithless. It is for the person who is dealing with addiction and the person who is sober. The gospel is for every person, no matter their past, no matter their background, and no matter their current status. No one should be left out. No one. I had to learn that one person matters – each and every person.

I truly believe that when we learn how important every single person is to our Lord, He will entrust others to us. When we see and comprehend how much God values one person, He will send others to us. But no matter how many He sends our way, we cannot lose sight of the fact that the one always comes before one hundred.

> *I tell you, in the same way, there is joy in the presence of God's angels over one sinner who repents.*
>
> Luke 15:10

CHAPTER TEN

Leading with Authenticity Is Better Than Leading with Authority

We had only lived in New York for a few weeks when we ventured out to our first Long Island pizzeria. When the guy behind the counter asked Jenna for her order, Jenna innocently asked, "Do y'all have just plain cheese pizza?" Without missing a beat, the guy said, "First, we don't say y'all. Second, it's called a regular." I do not think that Jenna has said "y'all" or "plain cheese" since then.

In all seriousness, I have come to love and appreciate the sincerity, honesty, and bluntness of New Yorkers. I have also come to realize and understand that people need and appreciate authenticity from their pastor. The adage of "they don't care how much you know, until they know much you care" rings true.

When it comes to talking about the gospel, the question is not always whether or not it is true, biblical, or accurate. Many times, the question revolves around wanting to know what the gospel actually looks like in our lives. I have learned that it is often easier to make emphatic statements with "thus saith the Lord" authority than to vulnerably lead with authenticity. And there have been plenty of times when I have needed to be transparent and real when I wanted to pretend that I had all of the answers.

However, I did not have all of the answers. More accurately, I do not have all of the answers. Jana Jenkins, a founding member of Crossroads, once shared with our small group that God had revealed a profound statement to her: "God cannot have a relationship with the person that you pretend be, but He can have a relationship with you." I will never forget that sentence for the rest of my life.

I never intend to be a fraud, nor do I intentionally deceive others in order to try and appear to be something that I am not. But, I have come to understand and appreciate that when I struggle, which I do, it is important to admit this.

I have come learn and appreciate that leading with authenticity is always better than leading with authority. Pretending to have all the answers does not help. Furthermore, acting like I have graduated from my need for grace does not help. Instead of leading with authority, we can confess our need and proclaim the truth that God has met our need.

> *Therefore, I will most gladly boast all the more about my weaknesses, so that Christ's power may reside in me. So I take pleasure in weaknesses, insults, hardships, persecutions, and in difficulties, for the sake of Christ. For when I am weak, then I am strong.*
>
> 2 Corinthians 12:9-10

CHAPTER ELEVEN

"His Grace Is Enough"

When we moved to Long Island in 2006, I very much desired to start a church. I had a willingness to do whatever we needed to do to see a church come to life and take shape. The only problem was that I did not really know what to do. At least, I did not think I knew what to do. I was seeking the Lord and praying consistently. I was reading and consulting with others. I had ideas and people alongside me who were trying to help us establish this new church.

In the early stages of establishing a church, I was mainly focused on trying to find a building, facility, or location. We looked at several different locations to start our new church that consisted of very few people. We toured a hair salon that was available for rent for the low cost of $3,000 per month that we could use on a regular basis. Even then, I knew that opening a church in a strip center off of the Hempstead Turnpike was not the answer. It was humbling to me to not have the answer because it brought me a sense of desperateness and a sense of dependence.

One day, I sat at the Panera Bread in East Meadow during the lunch rush. There were people all around me. I opened up my Bible and read 2 Corinthians 5, and as I read the passage, I felt the Lord speaking to me about the love and grace that He has for all people, and I realized that I needed to change the way I was looking at the people around me.

2 Corinthians 5:16-20 reads:

> *16 So we have stopped evaluating others from a human point of view. At one time we thought of Christ merely from a human point of view. How differently we know him now! 17 This means that anyone who belongs to Christ has become a new person. The old life is gone; a new life has begun! And all of this is a gift from God, who brought us back to himself through Christ. And God has given us this task of reconciling people to him. 19 For God was in Christ, reconciling the world to himself, no longer counting people's sins against them. And he gave us this wonderful message of reconciliation. 20 So we are Christ's ambassadors; God is making his appeal through us. We speak for Christ when we plead, "Come back to God!"*

I was struck by verse 16. Paul writes that we no longer view anyone from a human perspective. We do not look at them from our point of view. Instead, as Christians, we begin to look at them the way that Jesus looks at them; and Jesus looks at them with absolute love, mercy, and grace.

If we are not careful, we can begin to look at people as a commodity. What can this person bring me or offer me? Even in the case of starting a church, we can see people as means to meet our needs rather than seeing them the way that Jesus sees them.

If we are truly honest with ourselves, we can easily see people as potential church attenders, potential ministry servers, and potential offering givers. But, none of those things reflect the way that Jesus sees people.

We no longer look at anyone from a human perspective. We no longer dwell on their past mistakes, their track record, their upbringing or their background. Instead, we regard them as people who God desires to make new. And we begin to ask the question, "Who cannot be made new by God?" This perspective changed my entire thought process about starting a new church.

I left the Panera Bread that day resolved to share the message of Jesus with people, realizing that God desperately loved all of them. I stopped trying to figure out where we would meet or who would be interested in helping us start a church and began focusing on the message that we had moved to New York to share.

It is easy to lose sight of the fact that God desperately loves all people. Even in New York City, where there are 23 million people who live within 75 miles of Times Square, we can forget about the individuals who are on our block, on our train, and on the subway. We can easily begin to ignore people, categorize people, and compartmentalize people. In turn, this leads us to behave with a lack of awareness and concern for people.

In planting and leading a church, it is so easy to get caught up in buildings, programs, and events. It is also easy to lose focus of the Message and of the individual person we are trying to reach with that Message.

One of the most important things that I have learned over the last thirteen years is that the Grace of Jesus Christ is enough for me and it is enough for every other person on this planet. I have learned that I am never beyond the reach of His grace and neither is anyone else. My life truly changed nearly thirteen years ago when I was praying and meditating on 2 Corinthians 5:19. I began to more fully understand that God has given us this ministry of reconciliation to let people know that their sins are no longer counted against them because of what Christ has already done for them. This verse changed my life, our ministry, and our mission. I began to understand that no matter what had been done in the past – no matter the sin, no matter the guilt – the grace of Jesus is bigger than the sin and the grace of Jesus goes beyond the guilt. And this message is for me, you, Long Island, New York City, and the whole world.

> *That is, in Christ, God was reconciling the world to himself, not counting their trespasses against them, and he has committed the message of reconciliation to us.*
>
> 2 Corinthians 5:19

CHAPTER TWELVE

God Works in Me Before He Works Through Me

God works in me before He works through me. This statement may seem obvious, but I have had to learn to intentionally spend time with the Lord each and every day. This may not be for the reasons you would think. It is not for the sake of ministry, not for the sake of the church, and not because I am a Pastor but rather because spending time with Lord is essential due to my personal need for Him and His personal love for me.

Spending time with the Lord was crucial for me to learn to engage the people and the situations that were around me. There were people and situations that I would encounter that I never could have imagined. Over the years, I have met with people in the midst of divorce, cancer, drug overdoses, and suicide. I have conducted way too many funerals for people that were far too young to die. It is only by spending time with the Lord regularly that we can be prepared to share the hope and promises that we have in Him. We must be ready to engage.

We have the chance and opportunity to meet people in all kinds of different places and all kinds of different ways. By spending time with the Lord, we grow more and more assured that these encounters are not random or happenstance. We recognize that God has orchestrated these meetings for the sake of making Himself visible to people and to give us the opportunity of sharing the hope of Jesus with them.

It is truly inspiring and encouraging to see how God sets these opportunities in motion, and it is incredible to see how God allows paths to cross and lives to intersect. But that does not mean that we are safe from becoming tired and fatigued in the process. We most certainly need to have our minds renewed on a daily basis.

In our world of social media, engaging can become somewhat burdensome and tiresome. Most days, I scroll through my feed on Facebook. There are typically funny videos, cute pictures, inspirational words, and life and status updates. Then, typically, there are the posts that are passionately for something and the posts that are passionately against something.

It could involve any number of topics and I have no doubt that you already know what they are. The debates and opinions expressed on Facebook are part of what demonstrates our personalities and individuality. We are all different in so many ways and there is an appreciation for the variety of perspectives. But, mostly, the debates and opinions expressed can be exhausting.

It can be tiring to read the ardent arguments over and over again. And it can sometimes be hard to navigate relationships, knowing just how adamantly you oppose a person's beliefs or how much they oppose yours. If we are not spending time with Jesus on a continual basis, we will lose sight of who we really are. We will let the words of others impact us and make us question our identity. And we will be ill equipped for the day someone criticizes us or opposes in some way.

The thing is, I do not really like opposition. I generally like people and I generally want to be liked by people. I do not want people to think that I oppose them, nor do I want people to oppose me. So, I tend to do a lot more reading about the opinions of others than engaging them in my own opinions. Maybe my lack of engaging is because I am not sure that Facebook is the place to engage. Maybe I am not sure it will make any difference. Maybe I am worried about how my words will be interpreted. Or, maybe it is simply because it is easier to not to engage.

In many areas of my life, I have been content to be passive on my opinions about certain issues. I regularly post about my own experiences with God, but, I am not usually the guy to comment my thoughts and opinions about certain articles, videos, or pictures for whatever arguments are being made.

The only problem with this approach is that I do believe that Jesus is the only Hope for every situation. I believe Jesus is the only way that we find life and ultimate love. You may be wondering why this is a problem. The problem is that this becomes complicated due to the variety of understandings and misunderstandings concerning Jesus, and to another extent, Christians.

There are plenty of ways that I believe Jesus has been misrepresented on Facebook. There are numerous ways that Christianity has been substituted for something less than being Christ-like. And there are countless inconsistencies about who Jesus is and what Jesus would do, trying to shift Him to prove whatever point and carry out whatever agenda. These misinterpretations and misgivings about Jesus and Christianity often leave me confused on my response. I anticipate the argument of someone who is questioning why I have better understanding of Jesus and definition of Christianity than anyone else. So, I continue to remain silent, and I do not engage.

I was scrolling through Facebook a while back at a Hampton Inn in Louisville. I was drinking my coffee, reading, and perusing Facebook. This was not too different than most of my mornings. Suddenly, the fire alarm started going off in the hotel. One lady in the dining area leapt to her feet out of sheer fear. Over and over again, to whoever would listen to her, she said "Is this real? Is this real!?"

To make a long story short, it was not real. There was no fire and there was no need to evacuate. But, I never moved in the first place. I quietly drank my coffee while the alarm blared on for another three minutes. I remained silent, and I did not engage.

But, I have to tell you, I am not sure this is the right approach. I do not think that every opinion about every subject matters on Facebook. Yet, I am convicted that followers of Jesus, including myself, must engage in our culture on and off of social media. Spending time regularly with the Lord allows us to be bold whenever the time comes to engage.

God, while working in my life, was also preparing me so that He may work through my life. Knowing Him in this way allows us to have our minds renewed and hearts transformed. We can then more readily proclaim the truth about every circumstance. Jesus is the only Hope for every situation. I do not mean Jesus as a figurine, Jesus as a band-aid, nor Jesus as a pawn to be played. I mean the JESUS – the "Way, the Truth, and the Life" Jesus; the "no one comes to the father except through him" Jesus; the "name above all names" Jesus; the "no other name under heaven given to people by which we must be saved" Jesus.

My concern is that my silence or that my lack of engagement will be mistaken for indifference. I do not have an opinion on everything. But I also do not want to live my life silent on the things that really matter. Recently, I read a biography about Rosa Parks, and I came across this quote from Edmund Burke that I have read before: "The only thing necessary for the triumph of evil is for good men to do nothing."

As a follower of Jesus, I do not want this to be said of me. I do not want to be silent when it is time to speak, and I do not want to speak when it is time to listen. Mostly, I want people to know that the mercy, the grace, and the love of Jesus exists for every situation and for every person. I want to speak up, speak life, and speak love. I still do not think that I must comment on every opinion expressed. Yet, I do want for all commenters to know that they are loved, that they matter, and that Jesus is our only Hope.

I have come to the place of understanding that if I am not regularly spending time with Jesus, I will disengage. I will run away from the situations that I should be running toward. I will not be prepared. I will not be ready to provide hope. Whether face-to-face or on social media, we must be prepared and equipped to reflect and share who Jesus really is.

God always works in me before He works through me. On a daily basis, I have to confess to the Lord that I am not God but He is God. I am not the Provider, but He is the Provider. I am not in charge, but He is in charge. I must establish and re-establish these truths on a daily basis. As these become more clear, I find that I am more readily able to be used by God.

> *Jesus told him, "I am the way, the truth, and the life. No one comes to the Father except through me.*
>
> *John 14:6*

CHAPTER THIRTEEN

Life Is an Adventure and I Would not Change a Thing

When we made the commitment to come to New York in 2006, we knew that we wanted to be used by God. We believed that God would and could use us, but, we had no idea what that would look like.

Months before we moved to New York, we were still trying to decide if this was what the Lord had for us. I felt like it was, but Jenna was more reluctant. Jenna and I talked about what it would entail, and there were some significant reservations. However, a few days later, Jenna came inside of our house in Houston after just reading her Bible devotional outside on our patio. She had just read a passage of scripture involving Moses. The devotion she was reading focused on how God was asking for our availability, not our abilities. This quickly became our theme. We knew that we did not necessarily have the ability to start a church start and see it come to life, but we did believe that God could use us.

Just a few months later, we made the move to Long Island. As we were unloading our items off the moving truck in Levittown, it became clear that our refrigerator would not fit through the door. We removed the doors to the refrigerator. We removed the front door of the house. But, our Texas-sized refrigerator was not going to fit in the house, no matter how hard we tried.

After arriving at this conclusion, I posted that we had a refrigerator for sale on Craigslist. I looked on the page to see how it was listed and then I saw another listing above mine. This listing was looking for someone to play beginner level golf and tennis. At the moment, I did not know one other person on Long Island beyond my wife and two daughters, and I definitely qualified as a beginner golfer and tennis player. I was certain this was exactly what Jenna's devotional from months before was referring to, but I was very aware that I lacked ability.

Ready to make myself available, even in terms of golf and tennis, I ended up meeting the guy to play golf. The next month we played tennis. The next month he invited Madison to his sister's birthday party. Over the next eighteen months, we regularly met to play golf, play tennis, eat dinner, and drink coffee.

All along the way, our conversations would usually turn toward a spiritual discussion. We would talk about Jesus most of those times. We would talk about our lives and talk about what was happening around us. One evening, eighteen months from the first time we played golf, we were meeting to eat at a restaurant in Levittown. The waitress approached us to take our order and I was ready, but, very quickly, my friend told her that we needed another minute. I was a little surprised and looked up from my menu.

Looking me in the eye, my friend started his sentence. He said, "Before we order, I wanted to tell you that I have decided to trust

Jesus with my life and ask for his forgiveness." I was blown away by this. I could barely contain my emotions. Growing up in church and attending more than a few Vacation Bible Schools and camps over the years, my first thought was that I should lead us in a prayer. But my friend thought otherwise. He told me that he could pray and that he wanted to pray. To this day, I still very much remember his prayer of confession, admission, and celebration as tears rolled down my cheeks.

As excited as I am to share this story, I can honestly say that I can take zero credit for this. I know that God spoke to his heart from a culmination of things that lead to that moment. I believe that God used our conversations in an instrumental way to reveal God's grace and His love.

Yet, when I rewind it all the way back, I see that God used a Texas-sized refrigerator to do something great. He took something that we never thought would ever once factor into anything and used it completely for His purposes and for His glory.

That is what is fascinating about following God. God is not asking us to have the answer to every question. God is not asking for us to be His defender. God is not asking us to evaluate who needs the gospel and who does not need the gospel. God was asking for our availability more than our knowledge or plans. And we learned that if God could use the availability of a refrigerator, he could use us as well.

We did not know what we were signing up for thirteen years ago. We had no idea. In reality, there is no way that we could have known or predicted all that God had in store or that we could have anticipated what life would look like thirteen years later.

We have made more than a few mistakes, and there are some things that I wish I could do over again. But, I would not change what God has done in our hearts and our lives. I would not change taking the first step on this journey. I would not trade what we have been blessed to experience in New York over these last thirteen years for anything in the world. And, even though I have discovered, experienced, and shared the grace of Jesus in various ways over the last thirteen years, I am not over it.

I have come to love and appreciate the ways God continually uses broken and ordinary people. I am not over the depth of God's grace for me, and this compels me to want to share the message of His grace with the people around me. I am more and more in awe at just how amazing His grace is in my life. I am more and more aware of how God's grace is enough for every man, woman, boy, and girl. I am continuing to grow in my passion for seeing lives changed and transformed by God's immense grace. And most of all, I have continuously seen that God's grace still changes, still amazes, and still transforms. And, God still uses people who are available.

> *But Moses asked God, "Who am I that I should go to Pharaoh and that I should bring the Israelites out of Egypt?" 12 He answered, "I will certainly be with you, and this will be the sign to you that I am the one who sent you: when you bring the people out of Egypt, you will all worship God at this mountain."*
>
> Exodus 3:11-12

About the Author

Sterling Edwards and his wife, Jenna, have four amazing daughters, one spectacular son in-law, and one incredible grandson. Sterling is a pastor and a church planting catalyst living in Conroe, Texas.

Sterling can be contacted at sterling.edwards@icloud.com

Trust Publishers House,
the trusted name in quality Christian books.

Trust House Publishers
PO Box 3181
Taos, NM 87571

TrustHousePublishers.com

www.ingramcontent.com/pod-product-compliance
Lightning Source LLC
Chambersburg PA
CBHW052207110526
44591CB00012B/2112